AF443119

THE WHISPERS SERIES

'ABOUT MY BEST FRIEND...'

by Eve Vamvas

Illustrated by Louise Barton

Nightingale

An imprint of Wimbledon Publishing Company
L O N D O N

One can do without people, but one has need of a friend.

Ch'nese proverb

Friends are a necessity. But a best girl-friend is a luxury. Who else listens to your stories, understands your mood swings, appreciates your warped sense of humour and doubles your wardrobe options?

A best friend commiserates at your low points and delights in your success. She provides free entertainment whilst simultaneously running a 24 hour support and advice helpline - keeping her mouth shut when required.

A best friend willingly takes on responsibility for your emotional well-being.

The personal feelings and stories shared here show just how much we value our best friends. This book takes an honest look at what we do with and for each other and the essential role that friendship plays in all our lives.

UNDERSTANDING

"When my ferret died, she helped me bury him in the garden with a plant as a marker. She understood how upset I was, even though she'd always hated the ferret."

"Knowing that she's my friend gives me the confidence to do and say things that I would never have the nerve to otherwise."

"**S**he lets me go on and on when I'm really boring."

"When I first met Ellie, I thought she was loud and pushy and made a mental note to avoid her like the plague. I later worked out that I could be described in much the same way and that I actually quite appreciated those attributes. Now we are loud and pushy together."

"**S**he comforts me in times of need and aerobic classes."

"**S**he likes the same things I like and can bitch about all the things I hate too."

"When my best friend asks after my PMT I appreciate her understanding. If my boyfriend does I go absolutely mad."

"The best part about knowing each other so well is your attitude to each other's moods. I find it reassuring when my friend snaps at me, because she trusts me enough to show how she's feeling. And there's also a good chance that I'm about to get the complete story..."

II**W**e were both real tomboys at school and became friends because all the other girlies seemed so bitchy and unappealing. We still tease each other now about wearing skirts and make up."

"**S**he's like a sister without my family's hang ups."

"**W**e don't have the same taste in music, food or clothes, but we still go out shopping, eating and dancing and have the best time."

"A good friend doesn't wait to be invited. She just turns up at the door, ranting about her latest pet hate or failed relationship."

"Paula had a quick fling with a guy that I then went out with for ages. When we split up, she told me all her opinions about him and I realised that it had taken me years to come to the same conclusions. Now I consider her to be an invaluable time saver and she vets all potential partners."

"**S**he knows where I'm coming from. I don't have to explain how or why I'm feeling what I'm feeling - she just knows."

"**I** love my family, but there are certain things that can only be discussed with a friend."

"**W**e have a whole range of private jokes. Something funny will happen, or worse, somebody says something to set us off. I don't even have to look at her to know what she's thinking, and then knowing that she's laughing about it and that we're in on it together makes us laugh even more."

"We're as close as two people can get without having sex!"

"We'll call each other to confirm lunch, get gossiping and then be late to meet each other."

"I can always rely on her to be late."

"**W**hen we eventually start to feel the effects of oxygen deprivation and stop talking, we can be together in complete silence just as comfortably."

"**I** can always rely on her for a smile."

"**S**he has qualities that I admire - sincerity, kindness and a healthy ego. Qualities that I hope rub off on me because we're friends."

"**W**e have a better relationship than anything I have ever experienced with a man."

"**W**hen I've been particularly stupid, she reminds me of all the clever things I've done."

"**W**e talk and talk for hours about anything and everything, but if you ask us what about, we both say 'nothing'!"

"She loves hearing all my good news as well as commiserating with all the bad."

"When you share thoughts, feelings and experiences you become part of one another."

"When it comes to my secrets, I trust her better than I trust myself."

"I'll see something in a shop or hear a record and know instinctively that my friend would absolutely love it. I suppose in a way I'm always thinking about her even though I don't realise it."

"We might go a long time without seeing each other, but when we do it's like we had lunch the day before."

LOYALTY

"There are certain aspects of her personality that could be intensely irritating, but in a funny sort of way I've come to cherish her little quirks."

"She made it a personal crusade to get me over my boyfriend, and didn't give up until I had."

"Good friends operate a Seesaw Support System - when you're down you get balanced up again by your friend and vice versa."

"**S**he doesn't get impatient with me - even when I'm being exceptionally dim."

"**M**y best friend is outrageously attractive - she's a real man magnet. I love her to bits but I knew there was a God when she got acne!"

"I did something very selfish and hurt her badly. She knew I was truly sorry, accepted my apology and never mentioned it again. I don't think I could have done that."

"I went to Australia to meet up with my oldest friend. She stood me up at the airport and only spent two days with me in the entire three weeks, moaning about missing her new boyfriend. I was livid at the time but now I'm glad that she's found 'the one' and I've forgiven her for being a selfish cow"

"When you lend a wardrobe favourite to a friend and it comes back stretched and ruined, you just hold your tongue. It's easy to find a new top."

"**S**he videos all our favourite programmes when I'm on holiday and then waits to watch them with me."

"**I** don't have to impress her or be hysterically funny. I can just relax and be myself."

"**W**hen we were at school, we were both invited to what we thought at the time was a really cool party. Her mum wouldn't let her go, so she stayed in doing my homework while I went. My penance was that I was bored stiff without her there."

"**S**he had a red hot date with a guy she'd liked for ages the same day that I got dumped. I phoned to wish her luck and found myself blubbing with self pity, so she cancelled and spent the evening with me and a bottle of wine. She was there when I needed her and it made the guy more keen - obviously!"

"She pinched my boyfriend - he was actually an ex, but it still felt like the most humiliating betrayal. I didn't speak to her for three days, until I realised that I missed her more than I ever had the boyfriend!"

"We fell out once. It'll never happen twice."

"**S**he is well acquainted with my personality defects and nasty habits and likes me in spite of them."

"I found out I was adopted when I was 14 and my whole world turned upside down. I didn't believe that anybody could possibly understand how I felt, but Lisa listened to me when I wanted to talk and didn't force me to when I didn't. She accepted me for who I was long before I did."

"She's the only person who can give me an honest opinion about my dress sense and make me laugh at the same time."

"**W**e know things abcut each other that nobody else does. I feel that I have a special place in her life and it makes me strong.

SUPPORT

"She gives the same advice as my mother - except she waits to be asked for it."

"When she tells me all her problems, I feel honoured that she trusts me that much."

"She tells me the truth - even when she knows I don't want to hear it."

"She taught me that even beautiful people worry how their bums look."

"We met through our boyfriends and soon discovered we were both miserable with them. It was really illuminating discussing it with her because not only was she having similar problems but she knew us as a couple. Many a heart to heart later, we supported each other through simultaneous splits. Now we get together and whinge about being single."

"I started a new job and had a nightmare first day - it was so bad I was seriously thinking of not turning up again. Rachel came over and told me all these work-place horror stories to cheer me up. She also told me that I was wonderful and my new employers were slow to recognise real talent. She knew exactly what I needed to hear and didn't let me wimp out."

"I rely on her to tell me what to wear and get me home after too much alcohol."

"She's always had a worse experience than I have - it never fails to cheer me up."

"**My** best friend won't hesitate to tell me that I'm doing completely the wrong thing, while understanding totally why I'm doing it."

"She's the best listener. Quite often she won't say anything and lets me come to my own conclusions."

"I was putting on a lot of weight and moaning constantly to just about anybody who would listen. After several months of this, Sarah finally told me to do something about it or just shut up. I must have been incredibly tedious for her to lose her patience, but it was what I needed to hear and she had the nerve to say it."

"She encourages me to believe in myself, but brings me down to earth with a bump when I need to be realistic."

"**M**y best friend is like my favourite outfit - she lets me know when I'm too fat and when I look fantastic.'

GOOD TIMES

"I had the most devastating perm. She ran around to my house with a large hat as I sobbed in despair and escorted me back to the hairdresser. At the time, she didn't laugh once."

"My parents think she is totally mature and responsible, but she's the most outrageous person I know. She's a great cover for what we really get up to."

"We went backpacking around the world together. It was the most amazing year of my life and I would never have done it without her."

"I'm useless with money and invariably broke. But she's really sensible and is always subbing me for unmissable nights out."

"When we were young and very silly, we put Caroline's hamster on the record player for a few spins and then put him on the floor to watch him try and walk. It makes me blush with shame to think about it now, but God it was funny at the time."

"I joined a rowing club where Kirstin was the star of the show - superfit, elegant and an example for us all. I instantly hated her but after six months I shaped up and made it onto the team, which was a real achievement largely fuelled by my dislike of Kirstin. So I decided to actually talk to her and we've been great friends ever since."

"I am completely tone deaf, but my best friend still goes through the trauma of doing karaoke with me."

"We bungee jumped together at 4 am - I stared death in the face on the end of a piece of knicker elastic because she thought it would be a 'laugh'!"

"**O**n our last day at school we got drunk on cider and decided to make an exit by streaking topless across the playing field. For some reason it felt like a rites of passage statement and we thought it was hysterical. Didn't feel too clever the next morning, though."

"We can act like six year olds together. Without her as my friend, the world would be a very mature and dull place to be."

"We used to pretend that we were John Travolta and Olivia Newton John in *Grease* and dance up and down Hayley's staircase. One night I dropped her on the fling finale and she split her head open. She lied to her parents and said that she'd tripped up so I didn't get into trouble."

'"We went on our first grown up holiday abroad at 17 and thought it was very amusing to break into a posh hotel at 2 am to go skinny-dipping in their roof pool. The management called the police and we spent a night in the cells, terrified that our parents and friends would have to launch a nationwide ribbon appeal to get us liberated.'

"**W**e used to get up to so much mischief and then embellish the stories for the rest of the gang, that now it's hard to separate fact from fiction."

"She's my partner in crime."

Acknowledgements

Thanks to all my chums who shared their profound (and not so deep) experiences and observations:

Chants, Leesee, Emma, Susan, Ellie, Katie, Emmy-Lou, Louisa, Keiren, Heidi, Siobhan, Claire, Sarah, Mel, Harriet, Gail, Mereid, Helen, Caroline, Lois, Anna, Rachel, Lucy and Jack, Mark and James who have the sense to have female best friends.